ARE MOUNTAINS GROWING TALLER?

Questions and Answers About the Changing Earth

BY MELVIN AND GILDA BERGER

ILLUSTRATED BY ROBIN CARTER

SCHOLASTIC REFERENCE

CONTENTS

KEY TO ABBREVIATIONS
cm = centimeter/centimetre
ha = hectare
km = kilometer/kilometre
km^2 = square kilometer/kilometre
km^3 = cubic kilometer/kilometre
kph = kilometers/kilometres per hour
m = meter/metre
t = tonne

Text copyright © 2002 by Melvin and Gilda Berger
Illustrations copyright © 2002 by Robin Carter
All rights reserved. Published by Scholastic Inc.
SCHOLASTIC, SCHOLASTIC REFERENCE, and associated logos are trademarks and/or registered trademarks of
Scholastic Inc.

No part of this publication may be reproduced, or stored in a retrieval system, or transmitted in any form
or by any means, electronic, mechanical, photocopying, recording, or otherwise, without written
permission of the publisher. For information regarding permission, write to Scholastic Inc., Attention:
Permissions Department, 555 Broadway, New York, NY 10012.

ISBN 0-439-26673-4

10 9 8 7 6 5 4 3 2 1   02 03 04 05 06

Printed in the U.S.A.   08
First printing, February 2002

Allan D. Randall: Expert reader
U.S. Geological Survey
Troy, NY

To Ellie and Tom, with heaps of good wishes
—M. and G. Berger

To my wife, Jan, and our children,
Amy, Tom, and Billy
—R. Carter

INTRODUCTION

Earth is always changing. Mountains are building up and wearing down. Continents are drifting and shifting. Some oceans are getting bigger; others are growing smaller. Volcanoes are erupting and earthquakes are cracking open the earth's surface.

Some of Earth's changes, such as the shifting of the continents, have been going on for millions of years. And some, such as volcanoes and earthquakes, usually happen in just a few minutes.

Long ago, many people thought the earth was held up by four elephants. It was said that earthquakes occurred every time an elephant moved. Today, though, we have better answers to many of our questions:

- What makes mountains grow?
- Why do volcanoes erupt?
- What causes earthquakes?
- How are rocks made?

This book explains the main kinds of changes that affect Earth. Go outdoors and see some of these changes for yourself. The awesome Earth is just outside your door.

BUMPING AND CRUNCHING

Are mountains growing taller?

Some are. Mount Everest, for example, is the highest mountain in the world. But it is still growing about 1 inch (2.5 cm) every year.

Mount Everest is now 29,035 feet (8,850 m) tall—more than 23 times the height of the Empire State Building. Twelve years from now, however, Mount Everest will be 1 foot (0.3 m) taller than it is today!

What makes mountains grow?

Movements of the earth's surface. Earth's surface, or crust, is divided into about 30 huge pieces of rock. Each piece is called a plate. The plates fit together like pieces of a giant jigsaw puzzle. But these plates are not still. They are always moving.

Sometimes two moving plates bump into each other. Their edges crunch together. The rocks push up. A mountain range, or group of mountains, starts to form. The plates keep pressing against each other. Slowly, the mountains grow taller.

When did Mount Everest start to grow?

Around 45 million years ago. The Indo-Australian plate and the Eurasian plate bumped up against each other. Slowly, the crunching started to push up the rocks along the edges of the plates.

Over time, the piled-up rocks created a range of mountains called the Himalayas (HIM-uh-LAY-uhz). Mount Everest is the tallest mountain in this range.

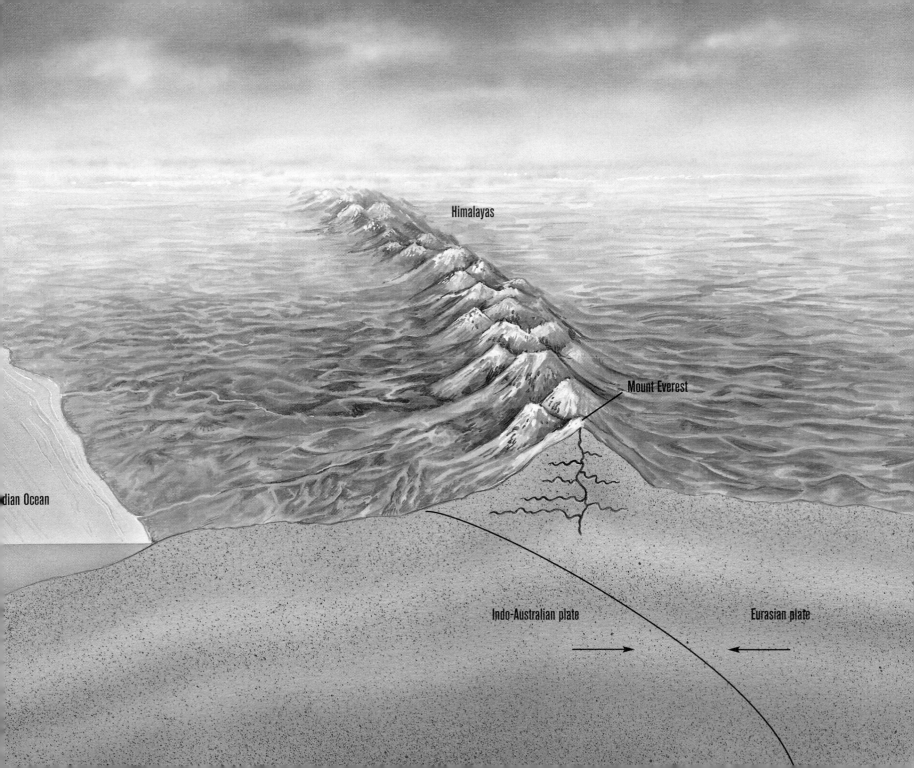

Himalayas

Mount Everest

Indian Ocean

Indo-Australian plate

Eurasian plate

What makes the plates move?

A layer under Earth's crust that is always moving. This layer is called the mantle. It is between the crust and the core at the center of the earth.

The mantle is so fiery hot that it actually melts rocks. The heat changes the rocks into a thick, heavy liquid called magma. The hot magma sluggishly churns and turns. As it moves, it carries the plates that rest, or "float," on top.

Do we feel the plates moving?

No, because they move too slowly. Scientists estimate that the plates shift only about 4 inches (10 cm) a year. That's about as fast as your hair grows. And you don't feel your hair getting longer!

Crust

Mantle

Core

Plate boundaries

How fast does the magma move?

Slowly. One scientist said that the hour hand on a clock moves 10,000 times faster than magma!

Are plates the same as continents?

No. Some giant plates carry both continents and oceans. Smaller ones carry just part of a continent or ocean.

Whether the top of a plate is a continent or an ocean depends on the thickness of the plate. You find continents in places where the plates are between 16 and 56 miles (25 and 90 km) thick. Where the plates are thin—less than 5 miles (8 km)—there are basins filled with water, or oceans.

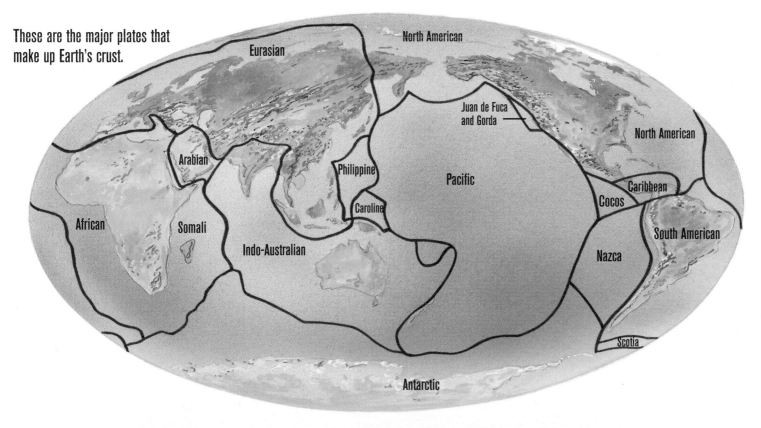

These are the major plates that make up Earth's crust.

Eurasian

North American

Juan de Fuca and Gorda

North American

Arabian

Philippine

Pacific

Caribbean

Cocos

Caroline

African

Somali

Indo-Australian

South American

Nazca

Scotia

Antarctic

What kind of mountains are the Himalayas?

Fold mountains. The name comes from the way the mountains are made. The plates under the Himalayas press together. They bend but don't break. The wrinkles and buckles form mountains shaped much like waves in the ocean.

To see how fold mountains are made, lay a heavy bath towel on a smooth floor. Place one hand near the center of the towel (one plate). Place your other hand near the edge of the towel and slowly slide that edge toward the center (the second plate). Notice how the towel bends and rumples into wavelike ridges (fold mountains).

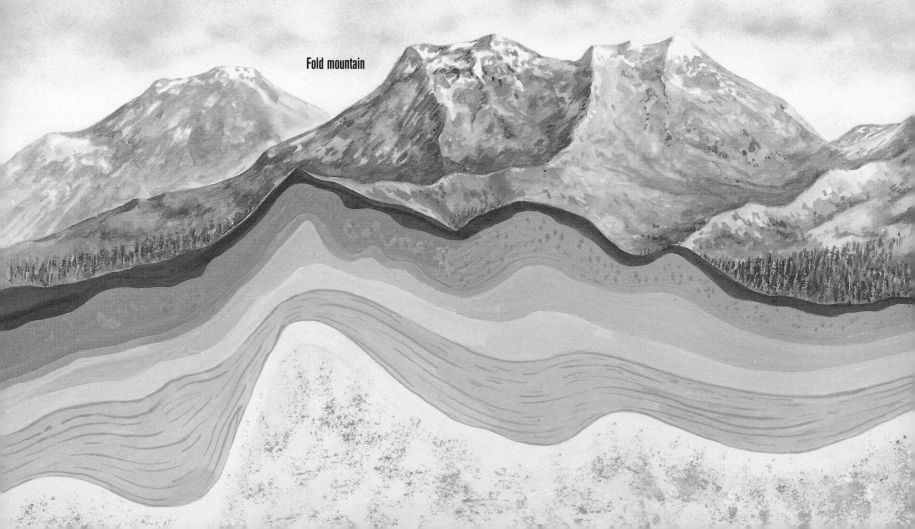

Fold mountain

Are all mountains fold mountains?

No. Sometimes two plates bump together—but they don't wrinkle or buckle. Instead, they thrust a giant piece of rock up into the air. Other mountains are formed when blocks of Earth's crust pull apart and one end tilts up. Mountains formed in these ways are called fault-block mountains. The Sierra Nevada mountains of California and the Teton Range in Wyoming are fault-block mountains.

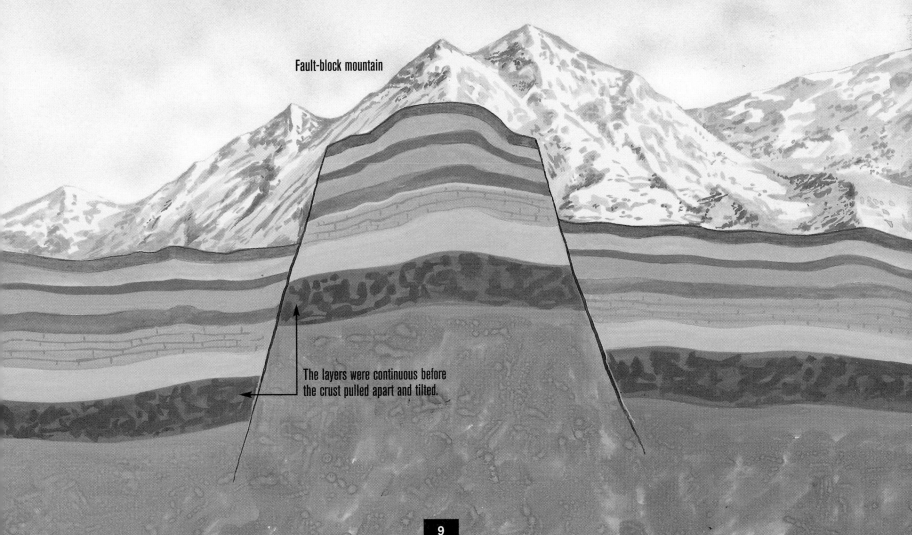

Fault-block mountain

The layers were continuous before the crust pulled apart and tilted.

9

Is the ocean floor changing?

Yes. Sometimes two plates do not push against each other. Instead, they pull apart. As they separate, they make deep cracks, called rifts, in the ocean floor.

What happens at the rifts?

Hot liquid magma slowly bubbles up from the mantle through cracks in the ocean floor. The water cools the magma. It hardens into solid rock. Occasionally, so much magma pours out in one place that an underwater mountain forms.

Where are the rifts?

In every ocean of the world. Scientists can tell where they are by looking for underwater mountains. In the Pacific Ocean alone there are about 14,000 such mountains.

Together the rifts and surrounding mountains make up the oceanic ridges. The best-known oceanic ridge is in the middle of the Atlantic Ocean. You may have guessed its name. It is the Mid-Atlantic Ridge.

How big is the Mid-Atlantic Ridge?

About 10,000 miles (16,090 km) long and 30 miles (48 km) wide. The Mid-Atlantic Ridge stretches along the entire floor of the Atlantic Ocean to the southern tip of Africa. The ridge roughly follows the shoreline of the continents.

Most of the mountains alongside the rift rise nearly 1 mile (1.6 km) above the ocean floor. Several peaks, however, are much taller. You see these mountaintops as islands in the Atlantic Ocean. Iceland and a group of islands off the coast of Portugal called the Azores are two examples.

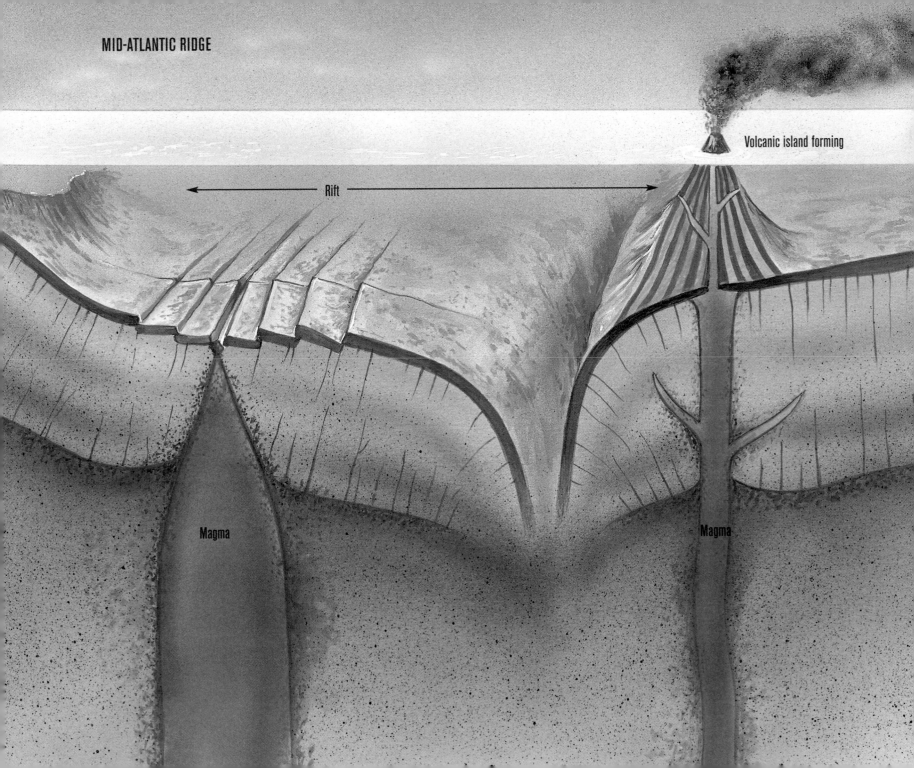

MID-ATLANTIC RIDGE

Volcanic island forming

Rift

Magma

Magma

THE OCEAN FLOOR

Gulper eel

Volcanic hot springs

Magma

Plainfin Midshipman

Clams

Tube worms

Hagfish

Sea cucumber

How does the Mid-Atlantic Ridge change Earth?

It makes the Atlantic Ocean wider. North and South America are moving west. Europe and Africa are moving east. As these plates separate, the rift or crack along the Mid-Atlantic Ridge widens. Magma squeezes up through the rift and hardens into rock. This heals the rift the way water from below heals breaks in the ice on a frozen pond.

Suppose you live in North America and have a friend in Europe. By next year you'll be about 1 inch (2.5 cm) farther apart than you are today. When you're old and gray, you'll have to travel a few feet (meters) farther to get together.

Is the Pacific Ocean growing wider?

No. As the Atlantic Ocean spreads wider, the Pacific Ocean grows narrower.

Is Earth's crust growing bigger?

No. The magma from the rifts forms new crust on one side of the plate. This side grows wider. But the opposite edge moves toward and slides under its neighbor. The forced-down edge slips into the mantle. The rock melts and turns into magma that comes up through the rifts and becomes new rock on one side of a plate. At the same time, rock is pushed down and becomes magma on the opposite side. The process goes on and on. The crust stays about the same size.

What are seamounts?

Underwater mountains. Seamounts rise more than 3,000 feet (1,000 m) from the ocean floor. But their sharp peaks do not reach above the water.

Seamounts seem to be quite rare in the Atlantic Ocean. But scientists have discovered several hundred in the Pacific Ocean.

What is rock formed from magma called?

Igneous (IG-nee-uhs) rock. The name comes from a Latin word that means "fire." This rock forms in the tremendous heat of the mantle. Granite and basalt are two kinds of igneous rock.

Are rocks made in other ways?

Yes. Some rocks are made from sand, pieces of larger rocks, and remains of plants and animals. Over millions of years, these materials pile up layer upon layer. This usually happens on the ocean floor.

The water and upper layers press hard on the bits and pieces. The pressure binds them together into solid rock. The process is like pressing snowflakes together to make a snowball.

Rock formed in this way is called sedimentary rock. Coal, limestone, sandstone, and shale are some examples of this type of rock.

Can igneous and sedimentary rock change?

Yes. Sometimes igneous or sedimentary rock move down into the earth's crust. Here they are exposed to tremendous heat and tremendous pressure. Over thousands or millions of years, the rock changes. Heat and pressure change igneous or sedimentary rock into a new type of rock called metamorphic.

The igneous rock granite, for example, becomes the metamorphic rock gneiss (NICE). And the sedimentary rock limestone becomes the metamorphic rock marble.

How old is the oldest rock ever found?

About 4.4 billion years old. That's plenty old. But it is not the age of Earth. Scientists believe Earth is about 200 million years older!

OLIVINE

SANDSTONE

GRANITE

BASALT

TUFA

COAL

GNEISS

LIMESTONE

MARBLE

MARBLE

AMBER

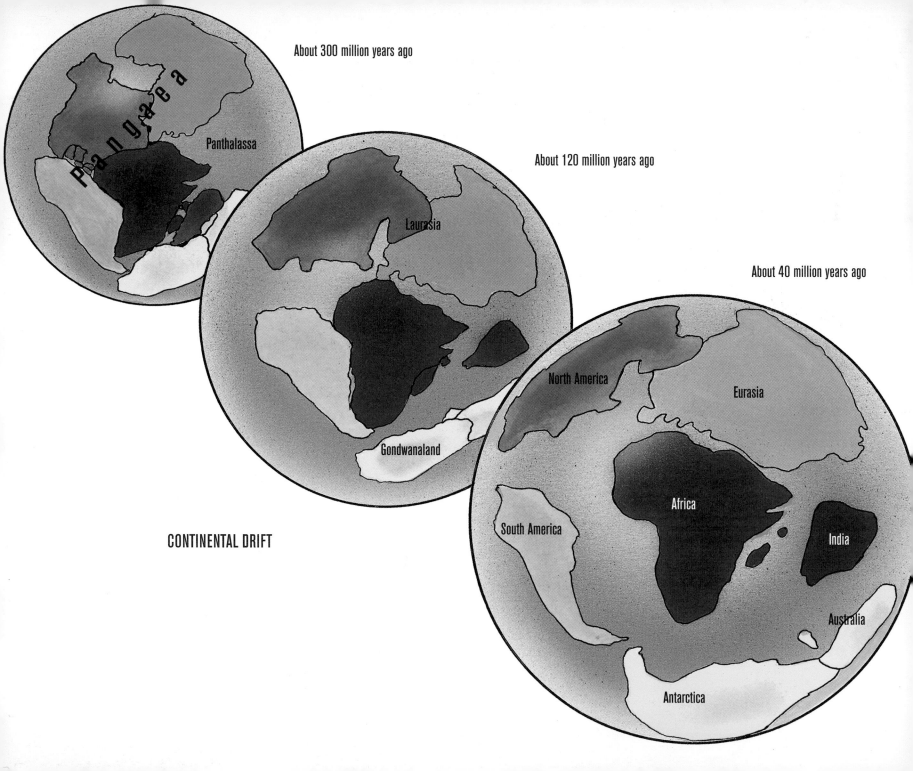

About 300 million years ago

Pangaea

Panthalassa

About 120 million years ago

Laurasia

Gondwanaland

About 40 million years ago

North America

Eurasia

South America

Africa

India

Australia

Antarctica

CONTINENTAL DRIFT

What did the continents and oceans look like millions of years ago?

Quite different from today. All the continents were joined together in a gigantic landmass called Pangaea (pan-JEE-uh). Pangaea was surrounded by one vast ocean called Panthalassa.

What happened to Pangaea?

It started to break apart about 200 million years ago. Eighty million years later, Pangaea had separated into two supercontinents—Laurasia in the north and Gondwanaland in the south.

It took 80 million years more for today's continents and oceans to start forming. Laurasia broke apart into North America, Europe, and Asia. From Gondwanaland came Africa, South America, Antarctica, and Australia.

How do we know the continents were once joined?

The shape of the continents is one clue. You can see how today's continents can fit together. The best match is between South America and Africa.

Scientists also have other evidence. They found fossils of tropical African plants and animals in modern Antarctica. This shows that these continents were once joined. And the same kinds of snakes, turtles, and lizards live today in both South America and Africa, which tells us that ages ago these continents were together.

Where will the continents be 50 million years from now?

No one is sure. But scientists believe the continents will continue to drift and change. In 50 million years, North and South America will have broken apart. Africa and Asia will separate, too. Part of California will break away from North America. Alaska and Russia may be connected. Antarctica will keep drifting to warmer places on the globe.

ERUPTING AND SHAKING

How do volcanoes change Earth?

They erupt and shoot out tremendous amounts of hot magma. The magma is called lava when it hits the air. The lava cools and hardens into hard rock, which adds layers to the earth's crust.

Pieces of solid rock also fly out of volcanoes. Many pieces are tiny, like fine dust. Sand-size pieces are called ash. Larger pieces are cinders, and the largest rocks are known as blocks. Some blocks can weigh as much as several tons (tonnes). And some pieces of rock, called pumice, are so light that they float in water.

What happens to the lava and rocks?

They pile up around the volcano. On land or under the sea, the lava and rocks grow into hills or mountains.

If the undersea mountains are high enough, islands appear in the ocean. Think of the Hawaiian Islands, for example. They are the tops of volcanoes poking above the surface of the water.

What makes a volcano erupt?

Pressure inside Earth's mantle. The force drives the thick, mushy magma into cracks or weak spots in the crust. Sometimes the pressure gets too high. The magma bursts out of the opening. Another volcano blows its top!

Which volcanoes look like upside-down ice-cream cones?

Small volcanoes made up of loose cinders with some ash and small blocks. Scientists call them cinder cone volcanoes. Sunset Crater in Arizona and Paricutín in Mexico are two well-known examples.

Which volcanoes look like upside-down saucers?

Those that erupt gently. Thin, runny streams of lava quietly pour out of craters, or openings on top of the volcanoes. The red-hot lava covers a large area. The moving lava slowly cools and hardens.

The rock makes mountains with broad bases and sloping sides. Because they look like ancient shields, the mountains are called shield volcanoes.

Mauna Loa in the Hawaiian Islands is a shield volcano. It is the tallest volcano on Earth. But it is not the highest. That's because its base, on the bottom of the Pacific Ocean, is 3.4 miles (5.5 km) below sea level!

Cinder cone volcano

Shield volcano

Are some volcanoes a mix of cinder cone and shield?

Yes. These volcanoes switch from eruptions of cinders, ash, and blocks to flows of thin, runny lava. The mix produces composite, or strato, volcanoes.

When you think of volcanoes, you probably picture composite volcanoes. They include some of the most beautiful mountains in the world. Mount Fuji in Japan and Mount Hood in the United States are composite volcanoes.

Are volcanoes still forming islands?

Yes. One famous island broke through the waters off the coast of Iceland in November 1963. Fishermen noticed smoke rising from the ocean. They thought it was a boat on fire. When they got close, they saw that it was steam from an underwater volcano.

After about four years, the island had an area of 1.5 square miles (3.8 km²). It stood 500 feet (152 m) above sea level. Icelanders named it Surtsey, after Surt, a Viking fire giant.

Can volcanoes destroy islands?

Yes. In 1883, a volcano erupted on the small island of Krakatau in the South Pacific. The ferocious explosion tore the island apart. It flung some 5 cubic miles (20 km³) of rock and soil into the sea. Krakatau shrank to only one-fourth of its previous size!

Can volcanoes shorten mountains?

Yes. Take Mount Saint Helens, for example. It is a volcanic mountain in Washington State. Before it erupted in May 1980, Mount Saint Helens stood 9,677 feet (2,900 m) tall. The volcano's powerful blast knocked 1,300 feet (400 m) off the mountain's top!

Do volcanoes ever cause mudflows?

Yes. Mudflows may start when rain follows a volcanic eruption. The water changes dust and ash to mud. The mud streaks down the mountain.

Mudflows also happen when hot lava melts the ice and snow on the peak of a volcano. The water turns the soil underneath into mud. And down the volcano it goes.

A tragic mudflow followed the 1985 eruption of the Nevado del Ruiz volcano in Colombia. The melting ice and snow mixed with dust and ash from the volcano. It made a torrent that plunged downward with a terrifying roar. Within five minutes, the muck buried the entire town of Armero with its 20,000 people.

The effects of an earthquake

Do earthquakes change Earth?

Yes. Major earthquakes may tear open huge cracks in the land. Cars and houses can tumble into the cracks.

Sometimes an earthquake pushes up sections of land. An example occurred 1,100 years ago in the present state of Washington. The quake pushed up a new 20-foot-high (6 m) stretch of land on Bainbridge Island in Puget Sound.

Earthquakes can bring down land, too. In 1811 and 1812, a number of quakes struck near New Madrid, Missouri. The severe shaking caused several small islands in the Mississippi River to sink under the water.

What makes an earthquake?

Usually the pressure of two plates pushing against each other. Sometimes small earthquakes occur at weak points within a plate.

Pressing plates can cause deep cracks in rock, known as faults. From time to time, one of the plates may jerk up, down, or forward along a fault. The sudden movement shakes the earth. It's an earthquake!

What is the best-known fault?

The 600-mile (960 km) San Andreas (SAN an-DRAY-uhs) fault, which runs north-south near the California coast. The Pacific and North American plates push against each other at the San Andreas fault. From time to time, the Pacific plate jumps northwest a bit. This produces a slight earthquake. In April 1906, however, the Pacific plate lurched forward a full 18 feet (5.6 m). The result was the very powerful San Francisco Earthquake of that year.

Can earthquakes make rivers and lakes disappear?

Occasionally. The ground shifts during an earthquake and can open holes in the earth. Such changes in the surface of the land can cause rivers or lakes to disappear. For instance, the Thames River in London went completely dry for a while during the Earthquake of 1158!

The effects of a landslide

When do landslides occur?

When an earthquake shakes the side of a hill, cliff, or mountain. The vibrations loosen the soil and rock, which slide down.

Sometimes the entire top layer of the ground gives way. It falls as one gigantic mass. Other times, the ground breaks apart. A river of soil and rock sweeps down. Major landslides cover everything in their path. They can completely change the landscape.

When did an earthquake and landslide move a river?

In 1959. A powerful earthquake struck southwestern Montana. It ripped off one side of a mountain peak. The split triggered a landslide. Tons (tonnes) of rock and soil crashed into the valley of the Madison River.

The debris formed a dam that blocked the water. Three weeks later, the water had risen enough to overflow the dam and carve out a new channel.

When did an earthquake and landslide make a lake?

In 1840. An earthquake in Kashmir shook the slopes of mountains above the Indus River. An enormous amount of earth and rock slid into the river valley.

The falling material created a dam. The water backed up and grew very deep. Finally, the dam formed a giant lake, 40 miles (64 km) long and 1,000 feet (300 m) deep.

Can earthquakes cause mudflows?

Yes. In 1970, an earthquake shook part of Peru in South America. The trembling knocked loose gigantic blocks of ice on top of Huascarán Mountain. The ice blocks fell and melted, triggering a colossal mudflow.

The mud slid down 2.5 miles (4 km) toward the valley town of Yungay. It carried tons (tonnes) of soil, rocks, and water. The sea of mud buried at least 18,000 people. When it hardened, the mud made a layer 33 feet (10 m) deep!

What are seaquakes?

Earthquakes that occur beneath the ocean floor. Seaquakes (and earthquakes, too) can build up towering, destructive ocean waves called tsunamis (tsoo-NAH-meez). Tsunamis race across the ocean as fast as 600 miles an hour (970 kph). When they slam into land, some are more than 100 feet (30 m) high. Tsunamis can knock over cliffs, wash away beaches, and destroy riverbanks.

A landslide can block the flow of a river and flood the land.

Landslide debris

BREAKING DOWN AND BUILDING UP

Are mountains growing shorter?

Some are. Over millions of years, mountains break down. Rain and ice eat away and split the rock. Fierce winds batter the mountaintops. Plants send their roots into cracks in the rock and break off pieces. Mountains lose an average of about 3½ inches (8.9 cm) every 1,000 years!

This natural breaking down of rock is called weathering. Rain, wind, and flowing water carry away the pieces in a process known as erosion (i-ROH-zhuhn). Together, weathering and erosion have covered the earth with big and small bits of rock.

Does weathering break down all mountains?

Yes. But remember that shifting plates raise mountains. Some mountains are pushed up faster than their peaks break down. That's why many mountains, such as Mount Everest, continue to grow taller.

How does rain break down rock?

By dissolving, or eating away, the rock. The water trickles down through cracks. Parts of the rock dissolve in the rainwater. It is just like salt dissolving in water, except that rain dissolves the rock much more slowly. Over many years, the rock starts to crumble.

Some rocks, such as limestone or marble, dissolve more easily than others. In these rocks, some of the cracks become tunnels. Streams of water start to flow through them. The streams may flow for many miles under the ground. Sometimes the tunnels become deep and wide. They form caves. The longest cave ever explored is the Mammoth-Flint Ridge Cave in Kentucky. It stretches more than 190 miles (306 km)!

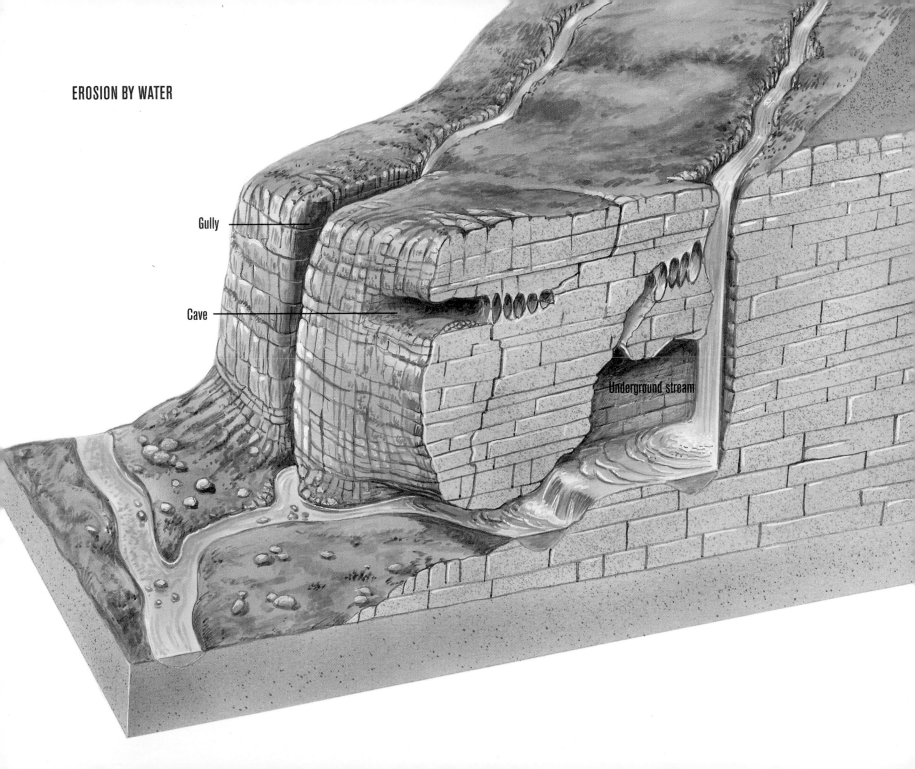

EROSION BY WATER

Gully

Cave

Underground stream

Rocks in the Sahara Desert are shaped by wind.

How does ice break down rock?

By expanding, or growing bigger, inside the rock. Rainwater seeps into a crack. In cold seasons or on the frigid peaks of mountains, the water freezes. As it changes to ice, the water expands and presses on the rock. Little by little, the ice splits the rock and breaks off pieces.

How does wind break down rock?

It blows loose sand and dirt against the rock. On softer rock, the flying sand acts like sandpaper. It makes rough and jagged rock flat and smooth. Or, it may carve rock into shapes that look like statues.

Sometimes air also breaks down rock. Oxygen from the air joins with iron in wet rock. The iron in the rock turns to rust. The rock becomes reddish-brown in color. Bits flake off—just like rust spots on old cars.

Can wind also build up the land?

Yes. In sandy areas, strong winds can pick up huge amounts of loose sand and pile it up in heaps or hills, called dunes. Sooner or later, the winds stop blowing, and the sand stops moving.

But the dunes do not stay in one place for long. When the winds blow again, the dunes move forward. They move in the direction the wind is blowing.

Dunes may creep along between 33 and 164 feet (10 and 50 m) a year. In time, "walking dunes" may bury a whole forest!

Does wind or water cause more erosion?

Water. Wind is only able to move the smallest bits of rock, such as dust and sand. But in places where there are not enough plants to protect the soil, the wind can carry away the best part of the land—the rich topsoil.

What is topsoil?

Usually the top 4 to 10 inches (10 to 25 cm) of soil. Topsoil is generally a mix of tiny bits of rock and the remains of plants and animals. It also contains small amounts of water and air.

In many places, there is a thick layer of soil on the earth's surface. Soil gives plants much of what they need to grow.

What happens to soil when it rains?

It can wash away. Long, heavy rainfall on a soil-covered slope can loosen the land. It starts flowing downhill. The rushing mixture of soil and water digs ditches in the ground. With each rainfall the ditches, called gullies, grow wider and deeper.

At the bottom of the hill, the rainwater and soil drain into streams. And lots of streams join together to make a river.

How do rivers change Earth?

They make valleys and help shape the land. Rivers flow downhill. The force of the water wears away the rock and sand in the riverbed. It slowly cuts valleys or gorges in the hills.

In time, rivers reach flatter land. They slow down. They also tend to wander. The rivers loop and curve from side to side. The older the river, the more loops it has.

The flowing rivers pick up lots of sand and mud. Finally, they empty into a lake or ocean. Then the water slows down even more. The sand and mud settles to the bottom. When the sediment builds up to the water surface, it forms a swampy plain called a delta.

How big are deltas?

They can be immense. The delta of the Mississippi River in the United States is over 10,000 square miles (25,900 km^2).

The world's largest delta is at the mouth of India's Ganges and Brahmaputra rivers. It has an area of about 30,000 square miles (77,700 km^2). What a big load of sand and mud these rivers carry!

River delta

How are waterfalls made?

Slowly. Most waterfalls start when a river flows over harder rock and then over softer rock. The water wears away the softer rock faster than the harder rock. This makes a step, or cliff, in the riverbed. The water plunges over the cliff, making a waterfall.

Waterfalls keep moving. Over time, the force of the water wears away the hard rock, too. And the waterfall slowly moves back up the river.

Where is Niagara Falls?

In the Niagara River, halfway between Lake Erie and Lake Ontario. Niagara Falls is about 10,000 years old.

Over the years, the pounding water has been wearing away the hard rock at the edge of the falls. The falls keep moving farther away from Lake Ontario. In about 25,000 years, scientists tell us, Niagara Falls will disappear into Lake Erie!

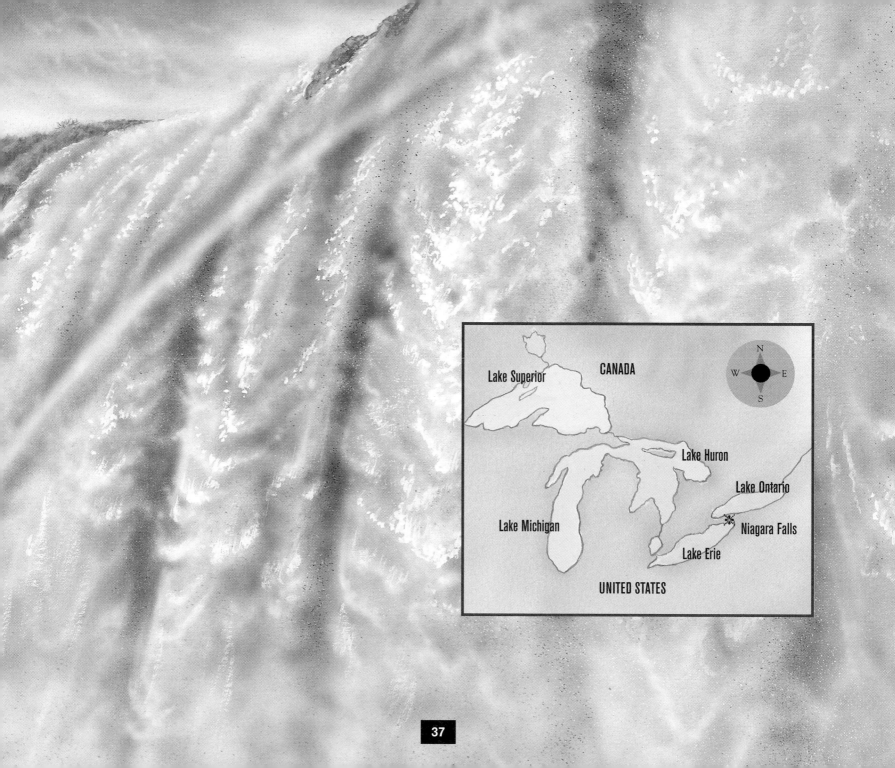

Lake Superior

CANADA

N
W ● E
S

Lake Huron

Lake Ontario

Lake Michigan

Niagara Falls

Lake Erie

UNITED STATES

Do oceans change Earth?

Yes. They shape the coastlines, which are where oceans meet the land. In some places the land slopes down to the water. Over time, heavy waves eat away at the shore. The gradual slope becomes a sharp cliff.

Or, the ocean waves may act like a huge saw, cutting away the bottom of a cliff. The water also flings boulders, pebbles, and sand against the cliff. This destroys more of the base. Finally, the face of the cliff falls into the ocean. We say the cliff has retreated.

The lighthouse on Martha's Vineyard, Massachusetts, sits on a coastal cliff. Every year, the pounding waves destroy about 5.5 feet (1.7 m) of the steep bank. Workers keep moving the lighthouse back. This saves it from falling into the sea.

Barrier beach

What makes beaches?

Waves. Moving ocean water picks up sand, lava bits, and ground-up seashells from the ocean bottom and coastline. Gently breaking waves drop this material along the shore. This makes a beach.

Big, powerful waves erode sand and rocks from cliffs along the shore and from the ocean bottom. They make the beaches larger. Sometimes this sand piles up as a sandbar or barrier beach. This long, offshore ridge usually rises 10 feet (3 m) or more above sea level.

What happens when there is too little rain?

The land may turn into desert. Deserts cover about 20 percent of Earth's land surface. The world's biggest desert is the Sahara in North Africa. It is almost as big as the entire United States!

Not all deserts are sandy, however. In many, the land surface is rock or gravel. In fact, only 15 percent of Earth's deserts are sandy.

Was the Sahara always a desert?

No. Over millions of years, the Sahara has been covered with ice, sea, forests, and grasslands. Dinosaurs used to live here. Egg and bone fossils found in the desert tell us that the land was once lush and fruitful. Imagine that!

What is happening to the Sahara today?

It is growing bigger. In recent years, a lack of rain has dried out the soil south of the Sahara. Many plants have died. Others have stopped growing. People and their animals crowd into very small pasture areas. When too many animals feed in one place, they destroy the plant life. The soil dries out even more. Each month the Sahara grows ½ mile (0.8 km) bigger!

What is a drought?

A lack of rain over a long period of time. Drought causes a shortage of water for use by people, animals, and plants.

Part of the United States suffered a great drought from 1930 to 1937. About 50 million acres (20.25 million ha) of farmland in the Great Plains region of the southwestern United States turned dry and dusty.

Huge clouds of dust covered whole buildings. The dust also hid the sun. It was dark even in the daytime. The region became known as the Dust Bowl.

Desert

Glacier

Where do you find glaciers?

In polar regions and on cold mountaintops. Glaciers are rivers or sheets of ice that slowly slide down mountains and across the land. The moving glaciers carve out U-shaped valleys. Most flow less than 1 foot (30 cm) a day. Others may cover more than 100 feet (30 m) in the same time.

Glaciers carry boulders, gravel, sand, and clay. Where the ice melts, the glaciers drop their loads. The "drops" form new hills and ridges.

Are there any glaciers near the equator?

Yes. Mountains over 20,000 feet (6,000 m) high near the equator may also have glaciers. The glacier on Mount Kilimanjaro in Tanzania, Africa, for example, is 200 feet (61 m) thick!

Did glaciers and ice once cover Earth?

No. Glaciers covered a large part but not all of the Northern Hemisphere during the last ice age. That period lasted from about 1.6 million to 10,000 years ago.

The Ice Age was caused by a drop in temperature. All of what we now call Canada, Denmark, Norway, and Finland, and most of the northern United States, Europe, and Asia, went into a deep freeze even though they were not entirely ice-covered.

Did the Ice Age change Earth?

It certainly did. So much water changed to ice that the water level in the oceans dropped almost 300 feet (91 m) and coastlines extended much farther out.

The glaciers of the Ice Age pushed soil and rocks before them, like giant bulldozers. This dug deep holes in the land. When the glaciers melted, these holes filled with water and some became lakes, such as the Great Lakes.

Do people change the land?

Indeed they do. People straighten rivers, flatten hills and mountains, dig canals, and much, much more. They dig deep holes, called quarries, in the ground, too. Here miners take out coal, metals, gemstones, and all sorts of minerals.

Copper miners in Utah, for example, dug one of the biggest holes in the world. It is 2.3 miles (3.7 km) across and ½ mile (0.8 km) deep!

Quarry

Do people help build up the land?

Yes. In Holland, for instance, the government built dikes to hold back the sea. The windmills on the dikes pumped water from the farmland into the ocean. This helped provide more land for farmers to raise crops. In Asia and in many other places, farmers build terraces on steep mountain slopes to catch rainwater and prevent it from washing away the soil. The flat strips of land are used for growing rice and other foods.

Workers plant trees to keep soil from blowing away. They also plant bushes at the edges of deserts. The bushes stop deserts from getting bigger.

Dike in Holland

What will Earth look like in 10,000 years?

No one is sure. But there's a good chance that rain, ice, wind, and plants will slowly continue to break down the surface of the earth and move cliffs and dunes. Rivers will dig great canyons. Oceans will remake the world's coastlines. Glaciers will carve new valleys. And people will change the landscape to fit their needs.

No doubt, the world will look different in 10,000 years. But we hope it will be just as splendid as it is today!

The Grand Canyon

INDEX

About the Authors

Outside the Bergers' front door there is a giant rock that a glacier deposited more than 10,000 years ago. "It serves as a constant reminder," they say, "of the awesome forces at work in our ever-changing Earth."

About the Illustrator

Robin Carter has been interested in illustration since he was a child. He has illustrated postage stamps, board games, encyclopedias, and many books. His favorite subject to draw is nature. Robin lives in Norwich, England, with his wife, Jan, their three children, and their golden retriever, Bella.